Messages from Salt Water

poems by

Sabrina Ito

Finishing Line Press
Georgetown, Kentucky

Messages from Salt Water

Copyright © 2019 by Sabrina Ito
ISBN 978-1-63534-970-2 First Edition
All rights reserved under International and Pan-American Copyright Conventions. No part of this book may be reproduced in any manner whatsoever without written permission from the publisher, except in the case of brief quotations embodied in critical articles and reviews.

ACKNOWLEDGMENTS

"Why I can never Trust a Woman," *Mikrokosmos (Mojo) Journal*
"Night Flight," *Bamboo Ridge*
"Climb," *West Trade Review*
"Sea Stars," *Santa Clara Review*
"Hiroshima Expats," *West Trade Review*
"Leaving Kamakura," *Caesura Magazine*
"Hafu," *Poemmemoirstory*
"So Much in a Gesture," *Slipstream Press, Witches of Lila Spring* (Plan B Press)

Publisher: Leah Maines
Editor: Christen Kincaid
Cover Art: Andrea Lee Tam
Author Photo: Amy Manso
Cover Design: Elizabeth Maines McCleavy

Printed in the USA on acid-free paper.
Order online: www.finishinglinepress.com
also available on amazon.com

Author inquiries and mail orders:
Finishing Line Press
P. O. Box 1626
Georgetown, Kentucky 40324
U. S. A.

Table of Contents

I. Center

Climb 1

Sea Stars 3

Hiroshima Expats 5

Leaving Kamakura 7

Burial 8

Night Flight 10

Hafu 11

Why I Can never trust a woman 12

Michael, with Blue Eyes 13

II. Peripheral

Koi 17

Fifth Date 18

Giggling at Bedtime 19

Seasick 21

Rideau Canal 22

Kamakura Bay 23

Porphyra 24

So Much in a Gesture 25

Fulford Harbor 26

Onryo 27

Leonids, and a Snowy Field 28

I. Center

Climb

Vines ensnare cliff face,
just as seaweed chokes rocks.

I have scraped knees
and bloodied toes
but because I always do
as I'm told,
I climb carefully,
don't look down.

Though, I can feel
the Pacific wake,
colossus at my back,
its thunder, its grating,
over shell-splayed floor.
I now understand
how water
grinds rocks
into sand.

I watch your fingers
reach up
to pluck
those tiny, dust-coloured globes.
'Sour grapes, they grow here
wild,' you exclaim, with boy-like wonder.

Their tannic acid rolls across
my rosebud tongue,
crushes to pulp
between my newly-cut teeth—
and I think they are
the most delicious fruit I have tasted
until now.

Sour grapes
picked for me
by my father,
hard won.

Sea Stars

If you cut off their legs,
they will just regenerate
and continue catching,
then sucking up
your fishing bait—
whether raw chicken,
salmon roe,
or sea worm.

mouth on belly,
spine on skin,
the wharves were plastered
with these mutant, purple stars.
And my father, the fisherman,
would curse each one,
chopping up at least half a dozen,
before even dropping a line
in the water.

but then there was that time
I was allowed to take one home
because I desperately wanted a dog
and it was thought, that a starfish
would suffice.

we brought one home in an ice cream bucket
I named the starfish, 'Roy,'
pet its bumpy back,
divulged all my secrets
and for four to five days,
watched him starve to death—
fade to beige,
soften to glue.

by then, even my father agreed
that it might be best
to bring Roy back to the bay.
he promised he would make a stop
on his way to office the next morning.

so, I sat at the kitchen window—
pressing my child hands
into the damp glass of morning dew,
which I blew out with my breath
to cloud the distant view
of my father walking away from me,
wearing his best brown, pressed suit
He carried Roy's ice cream bucket
somewhat gingerly,
though his car keys clanged
at his belt buckle
and his fishing knife bulged
from his back pocket.

Hiroshima Expats

Though it meant they had been safe—
shielded by the East China Sea
that clear, August morning, when white light
blasted away
even garden shadows,
vitrifying any hope
of an honorable return.

My father's family
were considered
traitors to Japan,
to the mutilated,
the pale-souled,
the destitute,
the suddenly mad,
the Dead.

For my father,
it was the gaunt-faced children
who self-segregated
to the back of the class,
pretending to eat rice
from their empty
bento boxes—
while the luckier ones,
like my father,
sat up front,
chewed discretely,
eyes forward,
stomachs rumbling.

He had been taught by his mother
to always glance back before leaving,
offer a half-bow,
utter his offering,

his unfinished lunch,
'help yourself, *dozo*[1].'

But, it was soul-killing just the same—
those children's eyes,

downcast,
performing deep, grateful bows,
waiting for their classmates
to leave—
so they could privately clamor
for those few bites of rice,
or whatever a seven year old,
himself starving,
had been willing
to share.

To have lived through all that,
my father's generation.

What they must carry in their hearts, like a drum—

for my father, it still keeps perfect time—
I am a traitor, I am a traitor, I am a traitor.

---

[1] Japanese word for, 'please'

Leaving Kamakura

The only walk I ever took with Obachan[1]
        was when I was four   and she was two years from death.

She wanted to walk up the hillside   to show me her town
        since I was moving to Canada   and had never seen it before.

We shuffled up the pebbly path steaming into late afternoon
        tiny houses seemed to crumble   under their clay corrugated roofs
the amber sun   hung   heavy   on our shoulders

        ('Gambatei[2]' Obachan hissed, through her gold-capped teeth)

But   my child   hand   was smothered by hers
       all flesh   and paper   and cold

and she tugged me at my elbow   too hard   and too high
       so that when we finally reached   the top
                    we were both shaking
                              and out of breath.

[1]Japanese for 'grandmother'
[2]Japanese for 'carry on' or 'persevere'

Burial

baby bird wings,
feather-frothed—

she breaks them off,
arranges them
wreath-like,
over the dead,
Dusky Thrush.

little girl fingers,
chilblained, red
pry back the seed-sized
lids of the dead
baby bird,
his eyes
like rice paper film
of sliding Shoji screens,
sealing
and concealing,
the Spirit World.

that she could only step
through those milk-veiled eyes,
cross bulbous rain,
ascend blue-grey sky,
she might be allowed
to understand
how with one last warble,
one last breath,
a baby bird soul
can pass
through the hands
of a little girl.

so, she fits
the corpse neatly
into a matchbox,
clasps the lid tightly
with a thread

then with red icy fingers,
she closes coffin into earth—

leaves the garden,
those baby bird bones,
all those shallow graves,
unmarked.

Night Flight

En route from Japan, stretched out for sleep
across three empty passenger seats,

I am wearing my yellow pajamas
with brown soldier stripes on the sleeves.
I hate them. They are too big for me.
There are no bottoms.

As I pretend to sleep,
I grate my bare toes
against the tight tucked sheets
I am wrapped in—
the only thing that now,
smells familiar.

Not like the plumy scent of American-style coffee,
or the wispy veils of Marlboro smoke
that tap, tap, tap from thin, silver ashtrays.

There is strange music on this plane—
the engine rumbles like an upset stomach
I hear the whispers of my parents,
hushed and sad.

I remember how I pressed my cheek into the metal arm rest,
preferring the sting of its cold, the hardness of it.
Anything was better than what was to come.
The word was, 'immigration,'
though I did not know that yet.

Hafu[1]

    the cherry   blossoms on   this   street are   white
      in   morning   they   release   cloudbursts
  lucent   petals   cling   to   pale   cheeks
         like   love-starved   children

     I remember school-day walks to the bus-stop in Japan
the   pavement   flecked with   slick   buds
  how   I'd love to smash   out their bloom
my   pink Mary   Janes   ran   far   ahead
            of my mother

        Gaijin![2] Gaijin! fat, stupid girl!**

Yve's parents were French he'd wait for me like punishment
      his   flaxen   hair   his   dead   blue   eyes
he'd   drive punches into   my   ribs   arms and thighs
    bruise me   from   inside
       the whole   way   to   school

    but   I   was   grateful for the   silent conspiracy
  my   offering   generous   I   thought
I   was   good   at   staring   ahead not   crying
     just   pretend   that   I   was
           invisible

    Years later I   became a   Canadian
        and   made   mud pies in   the dirt
showed my Gaijin friends how to suck the poison out
   of   red   China   berries
         until   they were gleaming
           and shriveled
                and white.

---

[1]Japanese term for 'half-race'
[2]foreigner, or non-Japanese

Why I can never trust a woman

because whenever my father wanted to spend time with me, he would take me fishing—and, for some reason, going fishing was always treated in our house, like an act of rebellion against my mother—who never minded that I got dirty, or wore torn jeans. Sometimes, she would plan to come with us—though when she'd describe the fifty pound lunch she wanted to pack, or how she couldn't stand the smell of frying fish in her kitchen, we would bolt out the back door, wave triumphantly from the car.

then, after a full day of fishing and a bucket full of catch, we would come home to disheartened Mother—who fried up the fish anyway, and watched us eat—her mouth, a thin, tight line. And we would laugh and joke, and I would enjoy the fact that I was on my father's side, joining in on the ravings about the deliciousness of the fish, though not quite as good as the salmon berries we had picked and eaten for lunch.

but, the truth was, I found the fish quite bland and smelly. And the sight of my mother's hurt made my heart lurch. For some reason, I was determined to pretend otherwise. At least, that's how I'd like to remember it.

Michael, with Blue Eyes

'Michael,' she says, 'what happened to your eyes?
He looks up at her, surprised—
'I know, man. They used to be brown!'
He smiles, in the way that always killed her—
like how he'd appreciate a slick, new motorcycle,
or the breasts of some pretty, young girl.

He never could hold back when it came to full-sized bodies—
even now, as she is with him, in the coffin shop,
his stiff body sitting straight up—modeling, it would seem,
the 'Cadillac' of coffins in a 50s metallic hue.
Michael, with brown eyes, turned blue.

'I can't get over you in that get-up,' she whispers,
pointing at his skinny suit, his shiny, black boots.
'and with those eyes, you really look like a white guy.'

He stares at her slyly, sniffs the carnation at his lapel.
'Eye donor,' he chuckles, 'Worked out for everybody, didn't it?'

She wakes to the alarm tone, screaming—
thick, honey hues of morning sunrise
lavish and gel the walls.

She calls, and gets the machine
of course.

'Hello, this is Michael, I'm not in right now. I'm riding the Izu Skyline. The ground is on fire and the air is the sea I'm drowning in. Say a prayer for me. Leave a message. I'll get back to you.'

Beep.

II. Peripheral

Koi

They are not the kind
that respond to clapping.

They are not Carp,
but the sort that hides
under duck wings
to steal food pellets
thrown with intention
at the ducks.

They wiggle
like swimming piglets
through the water,
making pop, pop, popping sounds
with their fish gums
as they smack
the peat-dusted
surface.

That they are safe
in this garden pond
at the Byodo-In Temple
is no question;
they are happy
to cool themselves
in the shade.
Though they hasten
from reflections
of our tall, masteous
shadows,
that would seem to
protect them,
but not Free.

Fifth Date

We stroll down Cornwall Street,
on our way to your apartment—
Pine trees and Yew trees
hang high above our heads,
their peppery scent gather
and mingle there—
mixing, with the sea-stained air.

Waking thoughts have no place
on nights like this.
Tonight, dreams will haunt
indifferent sleep—
celluloid versions
of hands clasped in smoke-filled restaurants,
arms locked, lip locks,
quiet caressing on the beach.

Did you know that the ghosts of uncertain lovers
live outside your bedroom window?
They were guided by the promise of softly lit journeys
through familiar, back-alley ways.
You grate your key into your apartment door
and I wonder-
        Is there a more honorable way in?

Giggling at Bedtime

For those looking for love,
I strongly recommend
finding someone with whom
you can giggle at bedtime.
Over something stupid,
ideally—that would have only
claimed smiles during the day.
But at night,
just before sleep,
its memory would cause
the giggles to bubble up
and erupt, into long-drawn pulls
of coughing, snorts and tears.
You would giggle so much that
words would be impossible—
though you'd try deep breaths,
then regress,
and giggle some more.

And when your stomach would hurt,
and your jawbones would ache,
and it would be well past eleven thirty,
so, enough already—
one of you would elect to be the grownup,
and say something boring like,
'We're just tired.
It's really not that funny, you know.'

And you would pull back from hilarity
and lay there awhile,
quietly regretting
as you wait
for the only alternative
to giggling now—
it comes sometime
between sharing
one last loopy smile
and crashing
into the bliss
of sleep.

Seasick

the medication hasn't helped /   not surprisingly / so, here i am / in this black hole / of a galley / fetal-positioned / retching / trying to / extricate myself / from my own core. /   i have given up / on gravity, completely. /   not the exact impression / i was hoping to make on your friends / during this three hour fishing tour / brim with beer, and / the steely dan band

i have to remember not / to be prejudiced, though /   not all white men think / women of Asian decent / are submissive / and have nothing to say / though, my wordless retching / offers little to defend / this stereotype / nor, you ducking in / every five minutes / to check on me

(I hear: pause / concerned whispers / muffled laughter / beer cans opening) /   meanwhile / i feel myself /   disappearing, /   face cradled / in cracked, orange bucket.

Rideau Canal

You took me to Ottawa to meet your Hungarian mother.
('It's a test,' my father said, 'an inspection leading to marriage.')
And though I thought it was all too soon, and too fast,
you wanted it that way,
and since I could never say, 'no,'
I got on a plane and flew past mountains.

When we arrived, I was sick for five days—
cringing at my fluttering hands, my self-conscious 'hellos'.
When the week was over, we went to Rideau Canal,
had our picture taken on a giant rock.
That's where I stumbled, trying to casually nestle into your arms.
I scraped my bare ankles, though from the photo, you can't tell
how I'd slipped, and you'd caught me
before I fell.

Kamakura Bay

The sun hangs
low and silver,
like a bell lamp
cupping the gun
metal sky.

I stand
at this caking lip
of seawall—
contemplating
young driftwood
and how easily
it frays,
under hard carves
of ocean breaks,
and stormy
days—

I realize
what it means
to surrender
to fragmentation,
then crash away.

In the distance,
baby seagulls
perilously ride
the spume.
They posture,
eyes scouring
for a buoy
to cling onto—
a life raft,
anything.

Porphyra[1]

forests in the sea
bed holdfasts, stipes and blades
of perennial sway,
pluming, fanning in the murk,
brown as ground seeds, green as play.

[1] species of seaweed grown on the coast of Japan

So Much in a Gesture

She watches, mesmerized, as he cuts the last bits of food on his dinner plate. It's the end of a familiar ritual for them: eating together, two old marrieds—placid, comfortable, expectant.

He waves his fork at the three bite-sized morsels remaining on his dish—steak, a bit of mashed potato, three peas. 'Isn't it amazing how that always happens?' he exclaims, bewildered by his own predictability.

And since there's not much she can say, she smiles, and admires how his fingers press deftly, manipulating the cutlery. She watches him gather the potatoes onto his fork (scrape), stack his peas (1, 2, 3) and then jab the last piece of meat.

He holds the fork up so she can examine what he's created: a montage of their meal, an orderly composite of 'things'.

He drops the food into his waiting mouth. She gets up to clear the dishes. Her back turned, she can feel his eyes on her, cold. Though he chews with exaggerated contentment.

Fulford Harbour

It is where we go for our evening walks
to hold hands
and throw sticks for the dog.

(Red jellyfish blot the shore here like blood-clots.
They die by the hundreds, on the shoreline.)

We race along fringes of water,
grinding shell to more infinite dust.

I laugh, though I breath you like sandpaper—

my fingers are splintered,

my throat septic,
        as silence.

Onryo[1]

Tell her she's broken,
        and she'll charge   through your nightmares—
                        sword-lashed,
                                  moss-frosted by night.
She'll smash all the china in the kitchen,
                trammel your infidelity into shards.

Then she'll scoop and self-cut,
        scoop and self-cut,
                until heart blood
      streams
    from her mouth,   and her eyes.

But before you can wake
from *her* nightmare,   she rides away—
                      spine humming,
                          under eclipsing moon.

                Even at forty,
                    when no lovers swoon.

---

[1] Japanese word for vengeful, female spirit

Leonids, and a Snowy Field

We follow the trail of headlights
that wind up the road to Cyprus Mountain.

It is three a.m.
and what was last week's snow
is this week's black ice—
and we are slipping all over it,
smashing our knee caps,
laughing like drunkards,
as we seek out
the perfect, lightless spot
to watch the Leonid's shower.

We settle on the middle
of a farmer's field—
private property, of course,
but this is a once-in-thirty-three years event—
and we are in perfect darkness now,
but for the reflection of the moon
on snow banks,
glowing,
as do our cheeks,
as do our eyes,
as we gaze with childlike wonder
at a million flashes, slashing up the sky.

And I look over at you,
and realize
that I want to stay here
and sleep off at least ten years of hurt—
wordless and reverent,
under this storm of cosmic litter,
healing from
the inevitability
of it.

Sabrina Ito is also the author of the poetry chapbook, *The Witches of Lila Springs*, released through Plan B Press. Her poems have appeared in numerous literary journals, such as *Clarion Magazine, Bamboo Ridge, West Trade Review, Slipstream Press* and *The Coachella Review.* A Simon Fraser University graduate, Sabrina has a Bachelor of Arts Degree in English and French literature, as well as a teacher certification degree through the British Columbia College of Teachers Federation (BCTF). Sabrina currently lives in Honolulu, Hawaii, where she works as an English and French teacher. A Pushcart nominated author, Sabrina has studied fiction, narrative nonfiction, poetry and screenplay writing for over ten years.

www.ingramcontent.com/pod-product-compliance
Lightning Source LLC
LaVergne TN
LVHW041512070426
835507LV00012B/1524